SLIME RECIPE BOOK

How to Make Amazing Slime at Home, Best Slime Recipes, Useful Tips and Tricks, Most Common Mistakes

By: Alex Hey

This document is geared towards providing exact and reliable information in regards to the topic and issue covered. The publication is sold with the idea that the publisher is not required to render accounting, officially permitted, or otherwise, qualified services. If advice is necessary, legal or professional, a practiced individual in the profession should be ordered.

From a Declaration of Principles which was accepted and approved equally by a Committee of the American Bar Association and a Committee of Publishers and Associations.

Table of Contents

Introduction

I want to thank you for choosing this book, "Slime Recipe book: How to Make Amazing Slime at Home, Best Slime Recipes, Useful Tips & Tricks, Most Common Mistakes" and I hope you find this book useful, informative and entertaining.

One of the latest trends and sensations to hit the Internet is the slime trend. Everyone is talking about slime, everyone is making it, and everyone is playing with it as well. Slime is extremely simple to make but highly entertaining. It is easily available on the market. However, it can be quite costly. But don't worry; this book will help you to make brilliant and quirky slime in no time.

Various kinds of slime are going viral on the Internet nowadays. However, most of this slime is quite difficult to make. It is also possible that a lot of things may go wrong while making slime, which may result in bad and unsatisfactory results. This book will help you make all kinds of slime with ease. This slime won't fail and will always entertain you.

The recipes given in this book are quite simple, and the required ingredients will be available at any drugstore and even in your home.

Along with recipes, this book also features various useful tricks and tips that will help you to make slime with ease. It also talks about the most common errors and problems that people face while making slime.

Once again thank you for buying this book and good luck.

Chapter One: Useful Tips and Tricks

In this section let us have a look at various tips and tricks that will help you make the perfect slime on your first attempt.

- Always wash your hands when you are done making slime. Similarly, it is also advised to wash your hands after playing with slime. A lot of slime contains substances such as borax that can irritate your skin.

- If you accidentally add too much liquid starch to your slime, lay it out on a flat surface and wait. After about five minutes the slime will become dry, and you will be able to re-knead it.

- Always use liquid starch with tacky glue. You can also use borax with tacky glue. However, it may take around a week to lose its stickiness.

- Do not use borax if you want to make a long staying slime or extremely stretchable slime. Borax should ideally only be used to make squishy slime.

- To make stretchy and durable slime use liquid starch.

- Add more food dye if you are using white glue to make slime. It will result in a brighter shade.

- Do not use superfine glitter while making slime. Fine glitter may work with clear glue; however, you must use chunky glitter with white glue.

- Superfine glitter, if used with clear glue without dye may result in stunning and unique slime.

- Add Pearl Dust to your slime to give it a pearly sheen.

- If you want to make magnetic slime, buy neodymium magnets beforehand. Magnetic slime will not work with weak magnets, and you must use extremely strong magnets to make it work.

- You can use eye drops instead of Borax to make slime. However, do not use eye drops with clear glue, as it will make the slime too hard and clunky. Eye drops can be used with white glue.

- Do not buy Orbeez and other such costly products; instead buy water beads from a local arts and craft store, or you can buy some online as well. You will get almost 10-times the number of balls for almost the same price or even less.

- Always buy a lot of glue while making slime. Try to buy gallon jugs instead of little bottles, as they won't last long.

- You can add nail art pieces and other such items to your slime to make it unique and beautiful.

- Use school grade glue while making slime, as it is cheap and very suitable for slime making.

- Making fluffy slime can be quite difficult. Do not add too much shaving cream to slime and add it sparingly. Too much shaving cream will make noodle-like slime.

- To make your slime fluffy, avoid using too much shaving cream, as it will make your slime like spaghetti.

Chapter Two: Most Common Mistakes

In this section let us see some of the most common mistakes and errors that people make while making slime.

Buying the wrong glue

You may be quite surprised to know that one of the main reasons why slime goes wrong is because of the type of glue used. Never use dollar store glue.

You won't save any money simply because your slime will not work. You must get good glue if you want to make good slime. You can buy glue from a good arts and crafts store, or you can find good quality glue cheap on various online stores as well. Online stores also offer a lot of variety and color options, often with huge discounts.

Not all glues are suitable for making slime. You must always use glues that contain PVA. If you use glue without PVA, your slime will turn out soupy and gooey.

It is necessary to buy a large amount of glue, as making slime needs a lot of glue. It is also better to have extra glue so that if you mess up, you can restart once again.

Measurements

Making slime is not rocket science. However, it still is a science. It is necessary to add all the ingredients in proper amounts if you want to make a nice, clean and perfect slime. People often tend to dump a bunch of ingredients in a large bowl and expect them to transform into a great slime. This may work once in a while. However, most of the time your slime will turn out to be terrible.

Unless you are a slime expert, do not dump a bunch of ingredients into a bowl; instead, try to follow all instructions given in a recipe properly. The recipes given in this book are simple and have clear steps and instructions. Follow them, and you will end up with perfect slime, every time.

Taking Shortcuts

Although shortcuts may be what people look for to shorten the time making slime, you should avoid them. Do not skip steps while making slime as it may mess up your slime and you may end up with terrible slime. You can follow certain tips that will make your slime the perfect slime. For instance always mix water and glue extremely well. You can use a whisk or another such instrument to mix the two ingredients.

Always add saline solution or liquid starch or borax in small amounts. Do not dump them in all at once. These ingredients are highly sensitive and if added, too much or too little may destroy your slime.

Saline Solution

Some slime recipes call for a saline solution. Saline solutions make making slime extremely easily. However, it is necessary to get the right saline solution. Buy saline solution that is buffered or has boric acid. The slime will not work if you do not use a buffered saline solution.

If you cannot find a saline solution with borax, you can use just borax instead. It will give the same results.

Too Much or Too Less Borax

Making slime with borax is quite easy. However, it may go wrong if you are not careful of the amount of borax you add to the slime. Do not add too much or too less borax to your slime. It is recommended to add it little by little. Too little borax can make your slime too stretchy and sticky whereas too much borax will make it too rubbery.

If you do make one of the above mistakes, don't worry. Just make another batch of slime and make the second mistake while making the batch. So, for instance, if you add too little borax in the first batch, make the second batch with extra borax. Combine these two, and you get the perfect slime.

Chapter Three: Basic Slime Recipes

Slime with Borax

Things you need:

- 2 teaspoons borax powder

- 1 cup Elmer's glue, clear or white

- 3 cups water, divided

- Food coloring of your choice

Instructions:

1. Pour 2 cups water into a bowl. Add borax and stir until it dissolves.

2. Add glue to another mixing bowl. Pour in water. Add food coloring until the color you desire is achieved. Mix until smooth and well combined.

3. Stir the borax solution into the glue mixture. Keep stirring until it starts to solidify.

4. Using your hands, bring together in a clump. It should be soft and moist to touch.

5. Start kneading the clump. In a while, it will feel drier and firmer. Throw away any excess liquid that may remain in the bowl.

6. Transfer to an airtight container or a zip lock bag, it can last forever.

Cornstarch Slime

Things you need:

- ¾ cup water

- 1 cup cornstarch (corn flour)

- 2-3 drops food coloring of your choice

Instructions:

1. Pour water into a small saucepan. Place the saucepan over medium heat until the water is just warm. Pour into a bowl.

2. Add food coloring. When the color you want is achieved, add a couple more drops (it should be a shade or two darker than the color you want or else the color will be diluted when the slime is ready). Stir using a spoon.

3. Add cornstarch to another bowl. Add the colored water to it add it slowly.

4. Mix into a thick paste using your hands.

5. If you find the slime mixture very watery, then add some cornstarch. If it is very thick, then add a little warm water. When you run your fingers into the mixture, it should move easily. Also, it should be dry when you touch the surface of the mixture.

6. Transfer to an airtight container or a ziplock bag.

Edible Slime

Things you need:

- 2 cans (14 ounces each) sweetened condensed milk

- Few drops food coloring of your choice

- 2 tablespoons cornstarch

Instructions:

1. Place a saucepan over low heat. Add condensed milk and cornstarch into it.

2. Stir constantly until the mixture thickens.

3. Add food coloring and mix well. Cool and play with the slime. You can eat it too!

Baby Powder Slime

Things you need:

- 1 cup PVA (all-purpose) glue

- 1 cup baby powder

- Few drops food coloring of your choice

Instructions:

1. Add glue and food coloring to a bowl. Stir until well combined.

2. Add baby powder and mix. Add more if required until the slime consistency is reached.

3. Transfer to an airtight container or a ziplock bag.

Powdered Fiber Slime

Things you need:

- 2 teaspoons powdered fiber

- 2 cups water

- Few drops food coloring (optional)

Instructions:

1. Add powdered fiber and water to a microwave safe bowl.

2. Add food coloring until the color you desire is achieved. Mix until smooth and well combined.

3. Microwave on High for 4-5 minutes. Keep a watch on the mixture so that it does not fall out of the bowl.

4. Remove the bowl from the microwave and set aside for 5-6 minutes. Stir now.

5. Repeat steps 3 and 4 a few times (2-6 times) until the texture of slime is achieved.

6. When done, let it remain in the microwave for 10-15 minutes.

7. Cool completely. Transfer to an airtight container or a ziplock bag.

Saline Solution Slime

Things you need:

- ¾ cup washable PVA glue, white or clear – up to you

- ¾ teaspoon baking soda

- 1 ½ tablespoons saline solution (the active elements in the ingredient list should be boric acid and sodium borate)

- ¾ cup water

- Few drops food coloring of your choice

- Glitters, optional

Instructions:

1. Add glue to a mixing bowl. Pour water. Mix until smooth and well combined.

2. Stir in the baking soda. Add food coloring until to the color you desire is achieved.

3. Add glitter and stir.

4. Stir in saline solution. Keep stirring until it starts to solidify.

5. Using your hands, bring together the clump. It should be soft and moist to touch.

6. Start kneading the clump. In a while it will feel drier and firmer and attain slime texture.

7. Transfer to an airtight container or a ziplock bag.

Dish Soap and Cornstarch Slime

Things you need:

- 4 tablespoons cornstarch
- Few drops food coloring (optional)
- Glitter (optional)
- 3 tablespoons dish soap or thick shampoo

Instructions:

1. Add dish soap to a bowl. Add color and glitter if using and mix well.

2. Stir in the cornstarch. Stir for about 10 seconds.

3. If you find the slime mixture very watery, then add some cornstarch.

4. Using your hands, bring together the clump. It should be soft and moist to touch.

5. Start kneading the clump. In a while it will feel drier and firmer and attain slime texture. When you run your fingers into the mixture, it should move easily. Also, it should be dry when you touch the surface.

6. Transfer to an airtight container or a ziplock bag.

Yogurt and Cornstarch Slime

Things you need:

- 2 tablespoons yogurt

- Few drops food coloring (optional)

- 6 tablespoons cornstarch

Instructions:

1. Add yogurt to a bowl. Add food coloring if using and stir.

2. Add cornstarch and mix well.

3. If you find the slime mixture very watery, then add some cornstarch.

4. Using your hands, bring together the clump. It should be soft and moist to touch.

5. Start kneading the clump. In a while it will feel drier and firmer and attain slime texture. When you run your fingers into the mixture, it should move easily. Also, it should be dry when you touch the surface.

6. Transfer to an airtight container or a ziplock bag.

7. Discard when it begins to smell strange or foul.

Psyllium Husk Slime

Things you need:

- 2 tablespoons psyllium husk

- Gel food coloring (optional)

- 2 cups water

Instructions:

1. Add psyllium husk to a microwave safe bowl. Pour water over it. Let it sit for a few minutes.

2. Stir and add color. Keep stirring until the color is well blended into the mixture.

3. Microwave on High for 5 minutes. Pause the microwave (when the mixture might fall out of the bowl.) When it settles down, continue heating. You may need to pause a few times.

4. This slime, when ready, is thick in consistency and gooey and jiggly to touch.

Liquid Starch Slime

Things you need:

- 1 cup washable PVA glue
- 1 cup water
- 1 cup liquid starch
- Few drops food coloring

Instructions:

1. Add glue to a mixing bowl. Pour water. Mix until smooth and well combined.

2. Stir in the liquid starch. Add food coloring according to the color you desire.

3. Keep stirring until it starts to solidify.

4. Using your hands, bring together the clump. It should be soft and moist to touch.

5. Start kneading the clump. In a while it will feel drier and firmer and attain slime texture.

6. Transfer to an airtight container or a ziplock bag.

Chapter Four: Favorite Slime Recipes

Unicorn Slime

Things you need:

- 2 bottles Elmer's glitter glue (6 ounces each)
- 1 tablespoon baking soda
- 2 tablespoons (up to 1 cup) water, optional if you like more stretching slime
- Pink, blue and gold glitter
- 3 tablespoons Contact lens solution (which contains boric acid)

Instructions:

1. Add glue and baking soda to a bowl and mix well. Add little water if desired, 1 tablespoon at a time if you like the slime to be stretchy.

2. Add glitter and mix until well combined.

3. Next add in contact lens solution slowly, mixing it simultaneously. Stir until the slime is formed.

4. Using your hands, bring together the clump. It should be soft and moist to touch.

5. Start kneading the clump. In a while it will feel drier and firmer and attain slime texture. When you run your fingers into the mixture, it should move easily. Also, it should be dry when you touch the surface.

6. If the dough is still sticky after quiet some kneading, then add some more contact lens solution. Continue kneading until it is ready.

7. Transfer to an airtight container or a ziplock bag.

Snowflakes Slime

Things you need:

- 1 cup Sta-Flo liquid starch
- 1 cup warm water
- 1 cup Elmer's white glue
- Snowflake table scatter, as required

Instructions:

1. Add glue to a mixing bowl. Pour water. Mix until smooth and well combined.

2. Add snowflake pieces and stir

3. Mix the liquid starch and keep stirring until it starts to solidify.

4. Using your hands, bring together the clump. It should be soft and moist to touch.

5. Start kneading the clump. In a while it will feel drier and firmer and attain slime texture.

6. Transfer to an airtight container or a ziplock bag.

Clear Slime (liquid glass)

Things you need:

- 2 teaspoons borax powder
- 1 cup clear Elmer's glue
- 2 cups warm water
- 1 cup water

Instructions:

1. Pour 2 cups water into a bowl. Add borax and stir until it dissolves.

2. Add glue to another mixing bowl. Pour water. Mix until smooth and well combined.

3. Stir in the borax solution into the glue mixture. Keep stirring until it starts to solidify.

4. Using your hands, bring together the clump. It should be soft and moist to touch.

5. Start kneading the clump. In a while it will feel drier and firmer. It should be stretchable, formed into a ball and should bounce

6. Transfer to an airtight container or a ziplock bag. It can last forever.

Fluffy Slime

Things you need:

- ¾ cup PVA washable glue

- Few drops food coloring of your choice

- 4-6 cups shaving cream

- 1 ½ tablespoons saline solution

- ½ teaspoon baking soda

- Little baby oil

Instructions:

1. Add glue to a mixing bowl. Pour water. Mix until smooth and well combined.

2. Stir in the baking soda and shaving cream. Add food coloring until the color you desire is achieved.

3. Stir in saline solution. Keep stirring until it starts to solidify.

4. Using your hands, bring together the clump. It should be soft and moist to touch.

5. Start kneading the clump. In a while it will feel drier and firmer and attain slime texture. Add baby oil right at the end.

6. Transfer to an airtight container or a ziplock bag.

Flubber Slime

Things you need:

- ¾ cup washable PVA glue

- ¾ cup water

- 6 tablespoons liquid starch

- Few drops food coloring

Instructions:

1. Add glue to a mixing bowl. Pour water. Mix until smooth and well combined.

2. Stir in the liquid starch. Add food coloring according to the color you desire.

3. Keep stirring until it starts to solidify.

4. Using your hands, bring together the clump. It should be soft and moist to touch.

5. Start kneading the clump. In a while it will feel drier and firmer and attain slime texture.

6. Transfer to an airtight container or a ziplock bag.

Hot Chocolate Slime (Non-edible)

Things you need:

- 4 ounces Elmer's glue

- ½ tablespoon Contact lens solution (which contains boric acid)

- ¼ tablespoon baking soda

- 1 tablespoons (up to ¼ cup) water, optional if you like more stretching slime

- ½ teaspoon cocoa, unsweetened

- Sparkly white glitter (optional)

- White confetti or small white foam pieces, as required

Instructions:

1. Add glue and baking soda to a bowl and mix well. Add a little water if desired, 1 tablespoon at a time if you like the slime to be stretchy.

2. Add glitter and confetti and mix until well combined.

3. Next add in contact lens solution slowly, mixing it simultaneously. Stir until the slime is formed.

4. Using your hands, bring together the clump. It should be soft and moist to touch.

5. Start kneading the clump. In a while it will feel drier and firmer and attain slime texture. When

you run your fingers into the mixture, it should move easily. Also, it should be dry when you touch the surface.

6. If the dough is still sticky after quiet some kneading, then add some more contact lens solution. Continue kneading until it is ready.

7. Transfer to an airtight container or a ziplock bag.

Chapter Five: Ideas for Making Fun Slimes

Galaxy Slime

Things you need:

- 1 cup clear glitter glue
- Acrylic paint (optional)
- 1 cup liquid starch
- Few drops food coloring

Instructions:

1. Add glue to a mixing bowl.

2. Stir in the liquid starch. Add food coloring according to the color you desire.

3. Keep stirring until it starts to solidify.

4. Using your hands, bring together the clump. It should be soft and moist to touch.

5. Start kneading the clump. In a while it will feel drier and firmer and attain slime texture. If it is not forming the texture you desire, add more liquid starch, a teaspoon at a time and mix well each time.

6. Add acrylic paint if using.

7. Transfer to an airtight container or a ziplock bag.

New Year's Eve Slime

Things you need:

- 2 teaspoons borax powder
- 1 cup clear Elmer's glue
- 3 cups water, divided
- Star confetti, as required
- Party beads (optional)
- Glitter, as required

Instructions:

1. Pour 2 cups water into a bowl. Add borax and stir until it dissolves.

2. Add glue to another mixing bowl. Pour water. Mix until smooth and well combined.

3. Stir in the confetti, glitter and party beads if using.

4. Stir in the borax solution into the glue mixture. Keep stirring until it starts to solidify.

5. Using your hands, bring together the clump. It should be soft and moist to touch.

6. Start kneading the clump. In a while it will feel drier and firmer. Throw away any excess liquid that may remain in the bowl.

7. Transfer to an airtight container or a ziplock bag.

Fluffy Snow Slime

Things you need:

- ¾ cup PVA washable glue
- 4-6 cups shaving cream
- 1 ½ tablespoons saline solution
- ½ teaspoon baking soda
- Little baby oil

Instructions:

1. Add glue to a mixing bowl. Pour water. Mix until smooth and well combined.

2. Stir in the baking soda and shaving cream.

3. Stir in saline solution. Keep stirring until it starts to solidify.

4. Using your hands, bring together the clump. It should be soft and moist to touch.

5. Start kneading the clump. In a while it will feel drier and firmer and attain slime texture. Add baby oil right at the end.

6. Transfer to an airtight container or a ziplock bag.

Ocean Slime (Non-edible)

Things you need:

- Liquid starch slime recipe
- Blue food coloring, a few drops
- Turquoise blue food coloring, a few drops
- Glitter, as required

Instructions:

1. Make 2-3 batches of the recipe each with the 2 different food colorings and one batch without any coloring. Add glitter to all the batches.

2. It can store for 2 weeks.

Christmas tree Slime

Things you need:

- 2 bottles (6 ounces each) Elmer's green glitter glue

- 2 tablespoons Contact lens solution (which contains boric acid)

- 1 tablespoon baking soda

- Red and green sequins, as required

- Green food coloring

Instructions:

1. Add glue, green color and baking soda to a bowl and mix well.

2. Add sequins and mix until well combined.

3. Next add in contact lens solution slowly, mixing it simultaneously. Stir until the slime is formed.

4. Using your hands, bring together the clump. It should be soft and moist to touch.

5. Start kneading the clump. In a while it will feel drier and firmer and attain slime texture. When you run your fingers into the mixture, it should move easily. Also, it should be dry when you touch the surface.

6. If the dough is still sticky after quiet some kneading, then add some more contact lens solution. Continue kneading until it is ready.

7. Transfer to an airtight container or a ziplock bag.

Conclusion

Thank you for buying this book, and I hope you found it informative, entertaining and enjoyable.

Slime is extremely fun to play with. However, not many people know that it is equally fun to make as well. This book features many recipes for a variety of slime that will help you enjoy the slime making process.

As this book has a dedicated section for tips and tricks and errors, you will be able to make perfect slime every time.

All the recipes mentioned in this book are easy to make and can be prepared by anyone, including children as well. However, it is recommended to have parental guidance when making slime as some ingredients may prove to be dangerous if ingested in large quantities.

Do not eat slimes!!!

Once again, thank you for buying this book and good luck.

Made in the USA
Monee, IL
20 November 2020